PLAYING TENNIS
WHEN IT HURTS

The cover photograph of this book is of Allen Fox, former member of the United States Davis Cup Squad and winner of numerous International Tennis Championships, including the Pacific Southwest Tennis Championships, the National Hardcourt Men's Singles Championships, and the National Intercollegiate Singles and Doubles Championships. In 1974, Mr. Fox was in a plane crash in Bolivia, South America, at which time he severely injured his back. Since the time of the crash, Allen has been "playing tennis when it hurts."

Cover photograph provided courtesy of Todd Friedman Photography.

PLAYING TENNIS
WHEN IT HURTS

K. Gordon Campbell, M.D.

Photographs by George Fry

CELESTIAL ARTS
Millbrae, California

CELESTIAL ARTS
231 Adrian Road
Millbrae, California 94030

First Printing, April 1976
Made in the United States of America

Library of Congress Cataloging in Publication Data

Campbell, K. Gordon
       Playing tennis when it hurts.

       1. Tennis—Accidents and injuries.   2. Tennis
—Physiological aspects.   I. Title.
RC1220.T4C35   617'.3   75-28753
ISBN 0-89087-155-8

   2   3   4   5   6   7   —   81   80   79   78   77   76

Contents

CONTENTS

Acknowledgments

The author is indebted to Ms. Diana Stumm, R.P.T. for her assistance with the exercise section and in demonstrating the exercises. Special thanks to Mr. Stan Scott, R.P.T. for demonstrating the taping and reviewing the exercise section. Mr. Dick Gould, Stanford University tennis team coach provided valuable information on injuries at the college level. Mr. Jerry Martin kindly provided the various tennis shoes illustrated.

Introduction

Tennis is a sport of movement, with sudden stops, rapid changes of direction, stretches and bends. To these are added the forces of a ball meeting the end of a long lever—your arm and the racquet. Hitting the ball well to prevent injury to the arm requires a transfer of force from the racquet, up the arm, to the shoulder and body. Faulty body mechanics in any part of your game leads to increased stress upon your bones, joints, ligaments, tendons, fascia or muscle. Inadequate strength of muscle or tight connective tissue will increase the chance of stress overload. This overload phenomenon can lead to pain, swelling, inflammation, partial tearing or even rupture of tissue.

Most of the problems discussed relate to what we call the "connective tissue," which binds the musculoskeletal system together. Examples are (1) *fascia,* the fibrous tissue around muscle; (2) *tendons,* which attach muscle to bone; (3) *ligaments,* which cross the joints going from one bone to another; and (4) *bursas,* little sacs with an oily fluid which have a protective function. All of these are prone to injury and become inflamed easily.

INTRODUCTION

With advancing age, there is an increased amount of "stiffness" in our connective tissue and an accumulation of wear-and-tear changes in our joints. There is a decreased capacity to absorb stress, and often a decrease in muscle strength, the major action system. Knowing that these changes occur, we must be alert to the various means of reducing the chance of injury, or the likelihood of developing an area of inflammation.

The first prerequisite is to keep connective tissue limber by daily stretching exercises. Any program must include the entire spine, the arms and legs. A good regimen takes very little time, but pays great dividends. A practical program for stretching, as well as strengthening and "warming up" is described in the exercise section.

A second prerequisite is to strengthen your muscles. Not only will this help to protect your joints and connective tissue, but will allow you to hit the ball harder, move quicker, and play longer with less fatigue.

If you have had a joint injury, increasing the muscle strength around it will reduce the joint workload. A well-muscled arm or leg may be the difference between playing or not.

General exercises such as running, cycling or swimming are excellent to build stamina and strength. Specific exercises are found in the exercise section. If you have a physiotherapist or trainer friend, ask for an individually tailored exercise program.

The third prerequisite is to "warm up" before playing. I don't mean just to rally, but to put your major joints through their complete range of motion several times and to loosen up the tightened connective tissue. This will change your body physiologically from a state of rest to one of action. *Rallying is not a substitute for warming up.*

By keeping limber, strengthening muscle and warming up well, you will avoid many of the problems discussed in this book.

A WORD ABOUT REST FOR INJURY OR ACUTE INFLAMMATION

The best initial first aid or treatment for acute injury or inflammation is: (1) elevation of the injured part, if practical; (2) application of cold packs or ice; (3) keeping the injured area quiet. All of this is *rest*. Sometimes a splint or cast will be needed. *Don't* use heat, and *don't* try to "work it off." Heat and motion have a definite role when the tissue is recovering or when the problem is a mild aching or stiffness.

The Neck

Wear and tear changes in and around the spine are the basis for most neck problems. Therefore, stiffness, aching or pain have a greater chance of occurring as the age of the tennis player increases.

The neck is particularly vulnerable during service and lob return, when the head is tilted back in so-called extension. The neck joints are actually compressed in this position. If there are wear and tear changes present, a setting exists for irritation, inflammation and the development of neck ache, stiffness or pain. With associated "disc" wearing, nerve irritation or "pinched nerve" can occur. This may be manifested by an ache or pain at a distance from the neck, such as around the shoulder blade, or down one arm. The more the neck extends, the more likelihood for the symptoms to increase.

11

If you have this problem, two changes in your game are needed: (1) play less forcefully and more relaxed, without as much neck and shoulder muscle tension (a relaxation exercise for the shoulder will be found under "Isotonic Exercises,")(2) change your service to the "hammer nail" type, where the backswing is reduced, the toss is lower, the tension is less, and neck extension minimal. Let the lob bounce, or stay relaxed and put a spin on the ball.

If changing your style of play doesn't solve your problem, give your neck two weeks of rest. Avoid as much as possible during that time the following: (1) sleeping on your stomach; (2) prolonged driving; (3) sitting at a desk or watching TV for long periods; (4) working with your head tilted back; (5) heavy use of your arms; (6) environmental stress. All of these positions and activities increase neck stress.

The most relaxing activities for the neck are: (1) walking, and (2) lying down with adequate pillow support. Hot showers and keeping the neck warm are helpful. A towel worn around the neck at night, or a soft collar while sitting and driving aids in rest.

Simple range-of-motion exercises can be done in the shower, but the muscle strengthening exercises should be delayed until the neck feels and moves well.

If symptoms persist, see your doctor for an accurate diagnosis, and the treatment program he can provide.

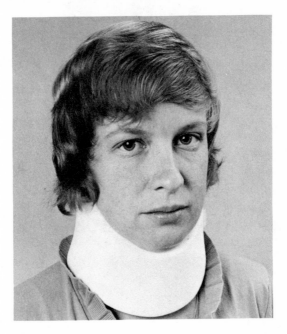

THE NECK

Shoulder

A smooth transfer of force from the racquet to the shoulder and body via the arm is the essence of good tennis. The shoulder assumes a great load with every stroke. Certain positions of the shoulder increase the likelihood of connective tissue irritation. This can occur by stretching or compression at the extremes of motion, or by overloading due to faulty force transfer.

The most common resulting problem is tendinitis. Compression or pinching of a tendon, particularly seen with the arm elevated as in serving, can irritate and inflame the tendon or adjacent bursa. Reproducing the motion reproduces the symptoms, so the problem persists. One can usually feel a sore point on touching the shoulder.

Rest or avoidance of the irritating motion will often serve as treatment. If the condition persists or recurs, changes in your game are needed. The "hammer nail" serve allows less tendon irritation. Keep your elbow close to your body during your strokes, and keep the grip below the level of the racquet face. Hit the ball at the lowest point possible, and if needed, don't follow through so high at the end of your backhand.

Often tendinitis symptoms really mean a more diffuse shoulder overload. The solution is to learn to transfer the force better, and this may require lessons from a professional. A smooth, fluid stroke should eliminate overload.

SHOULDER

Remember to warm up well, do daily stretching, and strengthen your shoulder muscles. This alone may solve your problem, and may prevent a secondary problem of "frozen shoulder" which occurs to some people after bursitis or tendinitis. You'll know if you have this condition, because of the decreased motion of the involved shoulder.

If the above advice doesn't work, consult your physician. After diagnosis, he may prescribe anti-inflammatory medicine, occasionally a cortisone injection, ultrasound, or specific rehabilitative exercises.

Arthritis of the shoulder joint may simulate tendinitis, bursitis, or overload. X-rays may be needed to make the diagnosis, so see your physician with a continuing problem.

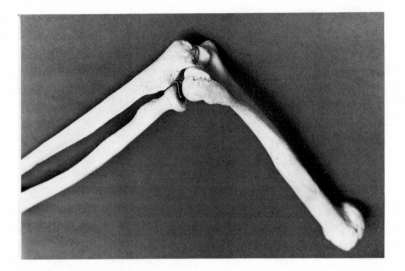

The Elbow

Mention the elbow, and the phrase "tennis elbow" comes to
mind. We know it commonly occurs, but we are not sure of its
cause. The term is nonspecific, and refers to an inflammation
of the connective tissue elements at the elbow, around the
bony prominences on the outside. Doctors use different terms
in describing the condition, such as tendinitis or epicon-
dylitis. The problem is one of overload, caused by the repeated pull and tug on this area of attachment, with resulting
irritation, then inflammation. The muscles which elevate the
wrist and fingers originate in large part from a small bone area
on the outside of the elbow, and these muscles are constantly
used and often misused in tennis.

ELBOW

The backhand stroke, particularly when not done well, with a bent elbow, jerking motion, late ball contact, and too much wrist action, can be the culprit. A serve with considerable wrist snap into flexion and pronation at the end (twist), or pronation with lateral bending (slice) can be your cause of trouble. A late volley with bent elbow and wrist snap is likewise damaging. A beginner is very susceptible to this condition, because of inadequate muscles, tight connective tissue, poor ball contact on the racquet, and jerky strokes.

As previously discussed, some people are more susceptible to inflammation of their connective tissue, just as others are more susceptible to ulcers or heart attacks. To counteract any such tendency, the player must have smooth fluid strokes and keep his musculoskeletal system in top shape.

Treatment depends on the severity and chronicity of the problem. For mild tennis elbow, a period of rest from tennis lasting two or three weeks will suffice. Not only avoid tennis, but also any activity which uses the muscles extending (or elevating) the wrist or fingers, such as carrying a heavy briefcase, hammering, hedge trimming, or even repeated handshaking.

The use of a tennis-elbow band offers relief to some if the condition is not too severe. The theory is that part of the loading is transferred to the band area and away from the elbow.

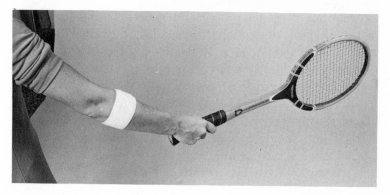

ELBOW

Treatment of the severe problem requires the use of anti-inflammatory medicine by mouth, ultrasound or occasionally a local cortisone injection into the inflamed tissue. The period of rest from tennis is prolonged up to several months. Wrist stretching and forearm strengthening exercises are used prior to the resumption of tennis.

There are several changes related to your tennis game which will help. Use a lighter weight racquet and move your hand up a bit on the grip. Change to a racquet which has greater spring. Reduce your string tension. Play less time each day or play doubles. Consult a professional to smooth out your strokes, and to learn correct force transfer. Reduce wrist motion to a minimum in all your strokes.

Warming up well before play is helpful, and daily stretching and strengthening exercises are a must, both as a preventive measure and to reduce the chance of recurrence.

If none of the above works, in selective cases your physician may recommend an operation on the elbow, the effect of which is to redirect the focus of force, and often to remove some of the chronically inflamed tissue.

Other conditions can give elbow pain. A similar condition to tennis elbow can occur on the inner side of the elbow, where the muscles which flex the wrist and fingers attach. This can be caused by too much wrist snap in serving and other strokes. These must be corrected. Treatment is identical to that for tennis elbow.

Another common problem is *synovitis* or inflammation of the elbow joint lining. It is manifested by swelling, stiffness, loss of joint motion, warmth and sometimes pain. It occurs because the joint has been used too much, and is more common if there are existing wear and tear changes within the joint. These changes are often secondary to problems experienced during childhood growth, such as "Little Leaguer's elbow," an inflammatory condition of the bone and cartilage. Old elbow fracture or injury, and overuse in athletics are other causes of early degenerative changes.

Rest and aspirin are used for initial treatment. Usually two weeks away from tennis will suffice for the mild problem. If the condition is more severe, chronic or recurring, consult your physician for a diagnosis and treatment program.

Other than lessons and reducing the amount of tennis, no changes in your game will be useful.

Occasionally less common problems occur, such as bursitis, other inflamed tendons, or pain from bone spurs. These also represent connective tissue inflammation and are associated with local points. They respond to rest, if mild, but may need treatment by your physician if more severe. What has been outlined for tennis elbow applies here.

The Forearm

There are relatively few problems encountered in the forearm. Occasionally the tendons on top of the forearm, one hand breadth above the wrist, become inflamed. This is a "crossover" point of two muscles and two tendons which rub one another during actions that require repeated wrist bending. When inflamed, the area will be tender, slightly warm and swollen. Wrist motion will aggravate the symptoms. Rest is imperative and generally will be the only treatment needed. You may return to tennis when the soreness is gone and wrist motion is comfortable.

A second problem is overuse of the pronator muscle in the forearm. This muscle is used to turn the wrist so the palm is down; this is used in the top-spin and twist serve. Soreness and tenderness in the forearm, one or two inches below the bend of the elbow, particularly when using the muscle, is characteristic. Limiting this motion is the only treatment needed.

Rarely a nerve gets squeezed below the pronator muscle as it travels along its pathway to the hand. Symptoms of grip weakness and hand tingling will occur. As with other nerve problems, this one demands a visit to your doctor.

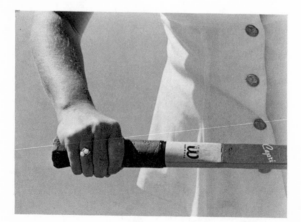

The Wrist

There are three major problems at this level: (1) tendinitis; (2) overload of the small joint between the ends of the two forearm bones (the radius and the ulna); and (3) inflammation of the wrist ligament on the little finger side.

All of these problems stem from excessive wrist action. Too much wrist flexion and rotation during the serve, hitting late on a forehand or in front or late on a backhand with wrist snap—all are irritating to the wrist.

Tendinitis usually occurs by excessive wrist rotation while bent. The small joint between the forearm bones is insulted by repeated turning of the wrist to the little finger side, or repeated wrist roll over in the two-handed back-hand stroke. The ligament is inflamed when the hand is turned to the thumb side, especially when the wrist is extended.

All of these conditions will be accompanied by an area of tenderness, and the faulty motion will reproduce the pain.

Rest is obviously needed but will only help temporarily. Correction of your faulty habits is essential. You also may need a lighter, more flexible racquet, or even a change in grip size. A slippery grip is disaster.

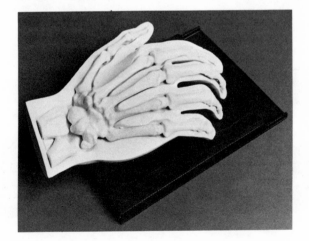

THE WRIST

A wrist band will remind you to avoid excessive wrist motion, but will do no more. Taping, if done correctly, does provide more support.

Exercises to strengthen the forearm and hand muscles are vital.

If you plan to include the twist serve, spin, chops and in general lots of wrist action in your game, expect some problem with your wrist.

(1)   (2)

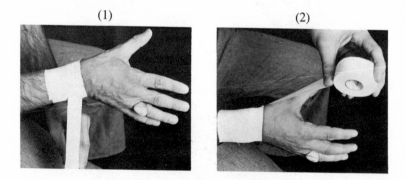

(3)

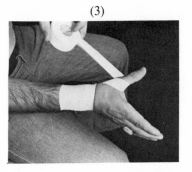

(4)

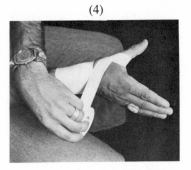

(5)

(6)

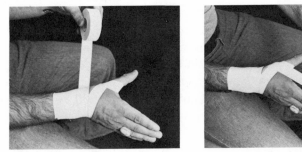

(7)

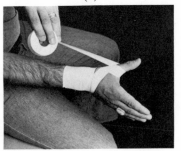

(8)

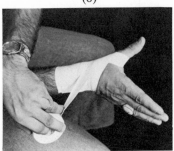

Four other less common problems can occur. The first is *synovitis*, a general inflammation of the wrist joint. Any joint can be overloaded and responds by becoming warm, swollen, stiff and sore. Rest is imperative to allow the tissue to "cool off." Aspirin reduces inflammation, and, if there is no medical problem with your stomach, may be taken two tablets, four times a day. For persisting symptoms, consult your doctor.

The second problem, which can occur with a fall on the court, is a fracture of the scaphoid, one of the eight wrist bones. Landing on the outstretched hand is the mechanism, the symptoms being those of a wrist sprain, that is, pain with motion, slight swelling and soreness. Unfortunately, many people shrug off this injury as a sprain with no treatment. The result is a fracture which doesn't heal, and painful, restricted wrist motion. It is therefore important to see your physician for any significant wrist symptoms after a fall.

The third condition is another nerve pinch or entrapment. Direct pressure of the grip on the base of the palm can cause the ulnar nerve to be compressed with symptoms of numbness and tingling of the ring and little fingers and weakness of grip. As with other nerve problems, see your physician.

The fourth problem is an inflamed ganglion. These are cysts, usually on the top of the wrist, and represent a mild localized degeneration of connective tissue. With increased use of the wrist, the cyst may become tender or increase in size. As a rule the cyst can be felt, and is often seen. If rest doesn't work, your doctor may try an injection. Persisting troublesome ganglia require surgery.

Hand

If your grip is correct, there should be little or no problems at this level. Any of the finger joints may become inflamed (synovitis) if undue stress is applied. I have seen this at the base of the thumb when a universal grip was used for both forehand and backhand. Rest and aspirin will work well, but if the problem is recurrent, your physician may want to x-ray your hand to rule out the possibility of arthritis.

Small cysts (ganglia) can occur at the base of any of the fingers, and be noticed as a small tender nodule irritated by holding the racquet. Treatment is by injection of the nodule with cortisone, or occasionally by surgical removal.

Pressure of the grip in the palm can irritate the underlying tendons. When inflamed, they can produce the so-called "trigger finger," which presents itself as a snapping or sticking of a finger as one tries to straighten or bend it.

To gain relief, there must be no pressure from any object in the palm. If the symptoms persist, local cortisone injection or even surgery may be needed. A softer grip or a glove may help prevent recurrence.

Occasionally, there are firm tight bands or nodules in the palm called *Dupuytren's contracture.* If you have any of these, gripping the racquet may cause soreness from the irritation. It would be wise for you to talk to your doctor about the degree of the problem, and to see if anything other than a different grip is needed.

Blisters are caused by friction, and some players are more prone to develop them because of their skin anatomy. By keeping the hand dry and the racquet grip nongreasy, these should be little problem. On hot days in may be important to keep a small towel handy to dry your hands. Or like the golfer, use a glove; or rosin, like the baseball player. Fracture and dislocations of bones in the hand can occur during a fall or by a direct blow of the racquet or ball. Any deformity or persisting sore area should be examined by your physician as some conditions require attention to prevent a permanent loss of function.

The Low Back, Pelvis and Hips

The Low Back.   Low backache or pain is a common problem in the general population, and tennis players are quite vulnerable. The nature of the sport places great demands on the lumbar area, particularly arching and twisting the back in service, returning a lob, and reaching out to hit a passing shot.

Existing degenerative changes in the low back joints, or the lumbar discs, accentuate any overload and lead to inflammation and pain. When irritated, the body tries to protect the area by a reactive tightness or spasm. This is manifested by an inability to get out of bed or a chair, a feeling of low back rigidity, and sometimes by such intense pain you feel

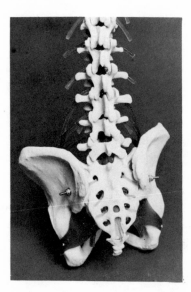 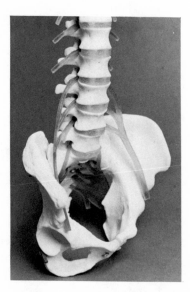

paralyzed. Milder forms take the form of stiffness, aching or pain with certain motions.

If a "slipped" disc is present, there may be pain, weakness, numbness, tingling or a sense of heaviness in the leg.

"Pulling" or straining a low back muscle is very rare, the problem is usually at the joint or disc level.

For all these pain patterns rest is important. The best rest position is lying down. Sitting or trying to keep going will only aggravate the condition. Mild heat to the low back and aspirin in regular doses are beneficial. With any symptoms of a "slipped" disc, or any continuing problem, consult your doctor.

You may resume your game carefully when the symptoms are gone, your back mobility is good, and you have resumed your other activities of daily living.

THE LOW BACK, PELVIS AND HIPS

Changes in your tennis game can be made and do help. Use the "hammer nail" serve to avoid back arching. Return the lob at waist level after the bounce. Don't stretch out for a passing shot. Play doubles instead of singles. Reduce your time of play. Warm up well.

Exercises are important for both preventive maintenance and treatment, so read the exercise section. Swimming, both backstroke and crawl, will not only increase back muscle strength but will also build more leg and shoulder muscle, while improving shoulder mobility.

Back supports of the elastic type or the more formal garment with stays are helpful to many people. They serve as a reminder not to arch the back or bend over too far.

With persisting symptoms, it is important to get an accurate diagnosis from your doctor.

The Pelvis and Hips.   Tendon and bursa inflammation, hip joint irritability, and partial tearing of muscle attachments to the pelvis constitute the major problems. All appear as a specific area of pain and tenderness, made worse by certain leg motions. Except for the tears, symptoms usually begin after play is over, and often not before the following day. Muscle attachment tears hurt immediately, and get worse with continued play.

The *trochanteric* bursa lies over the lateral prominence of the hip and is frequently inflamed. It presents a soreness at that point, worse with direct pressure, worse after sitting.

The various inflammatory conditions respond to rest, but may require anti-inflammatory medicine by mouth or even a local cortisone shot, if persistent.

The muscle attachment tears require only rest, but may take as long as six weeks to heal. Tennis should be resumed slowly after all aching has subsided.

No change in your tennis game will help prevent these problems, except perhaps to play less and not as vigorously.

Stretching and range of motion exercises for the pelvic area are the preventive program. Warming up well is imperative. Swimming is not only useful as a stretching and strengthening program, but can be done during any convalescent period.

With a persistent painful area, especially prolonged groin discomfort, see your doctor for a precise diagnosis.

THE THIGH AND KNEE

The Thigh and Knee

The Thigh.   The only notable problem in the thigh is a muscle tear. This can be in the front, usually the quadriceps, or behind in the hamstring group. By muscle tear we really mean a tearing of the fascial covering of the muscle or of the muscle tendon junction. Recognition is easy because the pain occurs at the time of injury, or shortly afterwards, if minor. Continued play with a fresh injury leads to greater tearing.

The minor tears are cured by a short period of rest. The major tears may be associated with swelling, discoloration, and considerable limp and pain with use of the leg. Rest may be required for up to six weeks, often supplemented by crutches or a cane.

Immediately after a major injury, ice is important to minimize swelling and reduce pain. After two days, wet heat is applied in the form of a whirlpool, bath or wet towels. Next comes an exercise program to maintain joint motion and muscle tone as comfort will allow. Swimming is helpful at this time. Stretching exercises are needed when the soreness leaves, because the muscle tends to shorten.

A good isometric and isotonic program is essential before resuming tennis or other sports.

The Knee.   Irritation of the joint lining associated with knee swelling is a frequent problem. This is what is commonly called, "water on the knee." The knee lining normally makes some fluid for lubrication and nourishment, but here it makes too much. All joints are subject to this problem, called *synovitis.*

This can occur in a knee joint that is overworked, but usually happens if there has been some preexisting wear and tear changes. With advancing age, all of us have some degree of joint wearing, perhaps made worse by an old injury.

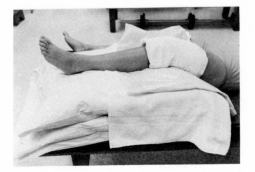

The condition may be present as a slight swelling and stiffness, or more dramatically by a great deal of swelling, considerable knee warmth, and acute pain.

Rest and aspirin will solve the mild problem. Swimming, whirlpool, a hot tub or warm compresses are all beneficial, *after* the initial period of ice.

A good warm compress can be made as follows: (1) wring out a bath towel in comfortably warm water and wrap it around the joint and adjacent leg; (2) cover this with a plastic "cleaner's bag" or Saran wrap; (3) cover the plastic with another dry bath towel. This pack will stay warm for thirty to forty-five minutes, the length of time needed for a complete treatment.

If the problem persists or recurs, see your physician for a more aggressive treatment program.

There is little to change in your tennis game except to give up singles, play less and slow down until the problem is resolved. Avoid lunging, sudden stops, and deep-knee-bend position.

As with all leg problems, the court surface is important. Clay and grass courts are kinder, but there is usually little or no option.

Developing more thigh muscle is important to protect the knee. This is done by strengthening the quadriceps and

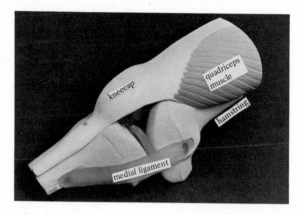

hamstrings. The isotonic program of progressive resistance (P.R.E.) is the best and can be done at home, in a gym, or a health spa. This is demonstrated in the exercise section under "Quadriceps." Be sure to note the change in exercise type if you have knee arthritis. Bicycle riding, swimming and hiking all develop these muscles, and can supplement the P.R.E. program.

Painful spots around the knee are also frequent, and are due to overloading, as we have seen elsewhere. They may be caused by inflammation of the tendons, ligaments, bursae or the joint capsule. The most common occur in the tendons immediately above or below the kneecap. The latter is called, "high jumper's knee." Other common areas for inflammation are in the medial and lateral knee ligaments; these often simulate degenerative changes or an early tear in a knee meniscus. Occasionally the hamstring tendons behind the knee or the posterior knee capsule will receive too much stress and become painful. These painful, tender areas are best treated by immediate rest and ice. After a day or two, begin heat in the form of warm compresses, whirlpool, or a hot bath. If the inflammation persists, your doctor may prescribe oral medication or occasionally a local cortisone injection.

There is no change in your game necessary, except to slow down. Knee supports are of no help except to act as an anchor. Thigh strengthening is important for future play.

The third and most dramatic condition is a torn or degenerating knee meniscus, the so-called "trick knee." Although much more common in the football player, it is also seen in the tennis player. There are two of these vulnerable cartilage structures in the knee, and either can tear or be subject to degenerative changes.

The degenerated meniscus may only express itself by symptoms of knee ache or pain. A torn meniscus may give one the feeling that something is slipping out of place. Occasionally the joint will "lock," that is, be fixed in one position so the knee has limited motion. This requires immediate medical attention. The milder complaints, if persistent, should be analyzed by your doctor. The torn meniscus can only be treated by surgery.

A few other conditions are worth considering. The kneecap may have a rough undersurface, due to wear and tear of its cartilage surface. This can produce aching, swelling and stiffness. Doing a deep knee bend with hands on kneecaps will often reveal the telltale grating sound. Although the condition can be diagnosed, it is often difficult to treat. In general, the knee is more comfortable if straight. Avoid whenever possible knee bending and other positions, such as sitting, with the knee markedly bent. These positions cause pressure between the kneecap and underlying bone, and this pressure aggravates the problem. Quadriceps strengthening is helpful to protect the knee and will therefore reduce the load on the knee, however, it must be done with the knee straight.

The kneecap may partially or completely slip out of its groove laterally. This usually occurs with weight on the leg, the knee slightly bent and during a change in direction. It happens to those who do not have a good anatomical relationship of their kneecap to its corresponding groove in the end of the thigh bone (femur). Because the condition relates to the way the knee is made, no lessons or altered style of play will help. A knee support will serve as a reminder, and in that sense may help. Strengthening the anterior thigh muscles will give the greatest protection. If the problem is chronic, you may have to give up the game. Surgery is helpful in some instances.

Tearing the attachments of the large posterior calf muscles from behind the knee is not uncommon. It occurs suddenly and is obvious because of the pain, tenderness and limp. Elevation, ice and rest are important to minimize further tearing and swelling. Crutches may be required. After two days, wet heat is employed. When comfort allows, a muscle maintenance program is begun, particularly swimming.

When the soreness is gone, a more aggressive program is begun. Calf muscle strengthening and knee and ankle range of motion exercises are essential. Jogging and running supplement the program. Wearing a ¼"-½" heel lift during the acute phase reduces the amount of stress on the injured tissue.

Knee instability from an old ligament injury is manifested on the court by a feeling that the joint is going to collapse or buckle. If extensive thigh muscle strengthening does not give relief, a metal hinged knee support can be worn and does help some players. Reconstructive surgery may be advised by your physician.

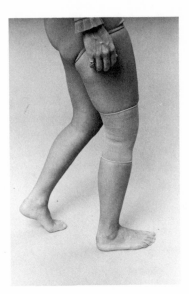
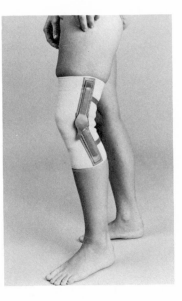

The Calf, Ankle and Foot

The Calf. The dominant problem in the calf is tearing of the muscle-tendon junction at mid-calf level. A large muscle, the gastrocnemius, can tear at its attachment behind the knee, but more commonly in the mid posterior calf. It may be a minimal tear, manifested only by a mild ache, or it can be incapacitating. Many players feel as though they have been hit in the leg by a racquet or ball. If a partial tear has occurred, and the initial mild symptoms of aching are unheeded, further tearing and more pain can follow. Signs and symptoms usually appear at the posterior medial calf, and may include muscle spasm, local tenderness, swelling, and increased pain with weight bearing. Swelling of the entire calf may follow within a day or two. Blood pigments may appear as a bluish discoloration in the lower leg.

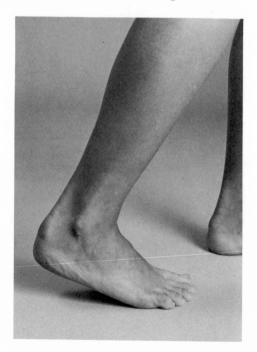

As with tearing behind the knee, immediate elevation and ice are needed to reduce further swelling and blood leakage. Heat to the leg during the first two days will make the problem worse. A cane or crutches should be used, if needed. An elastic wrap from the toes to the knee will prevent further swelling. A ½″ heel lift during the recovery phase lessens muscle pull, but as healing continues, a gradual calf muscle stretching and strengthening program is required.

As a means of prevention, a regular posterior calf muscle stretching program, as done by skiers, is worth the daily effort. Warming up well before play is likewise a good preventive.

Another calf muscle, small and unimportant, called the *plantaris,* may tear at its tendon junction and simulate a more major tear. Whereas a gastrocnemius tear may require six to eight weeks to heal, this muscle usually allows full activity in one or two weeks. At the time of acute injury, however, the two cannot be distinguished.

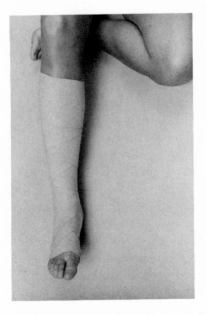

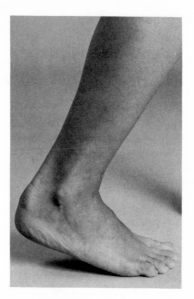

A tear of the Achilles tendon is a disaster. This large tendon attaches the posterior calf muscles to the heel. There is immediate disability with a limp and inability to rise onto the ball of the foot. Walking is therefore done flat-footed; running is impossible. Swelling and tenderness above the heel will be present.

This problem requires immediate medical attention, and surgical repair is usually necessary. The recovery time is prolonged, and tennis may be delayed for three to six months. If there is any doubt about your having this injury, see your doctor. Untreated, the disability is great.

Tendinitis of the Achilles tendon, or of the anterior tibial tendon, adjacent to the shinbone in the front of the leg, will cause pain and local swelling. Rest is required and regular doses of aspirin will solve the milder conditions. Stronger medicines may be suggested by your physician for the persisting or recurrent cases. Continued play will only make the problem worse.

The final injury is called, "stress fracture." It usually occurs in the small leg bone, the fibula. As repeated bending of metal can cause a fracture, so too can continual stress upon bone. Symptoms of aching with weight bearing may be the only clue to the problem. A common location of fracture is one to two hand breadths above the ankle on the outside. Persistent weight bearing will cause an increase in symptoms, usually more annoying than disabling. Diagnosis is often difficult, because the fracture is commonly not seen on x-ray for three weeks. Six weeks of rest from running is the only treatment required.

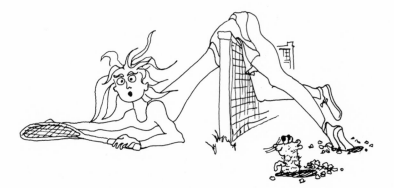

The Ankle. One immediately thinks of a "sprain," which indeed is the chief problem. The injury is termed mild, moderate or severe depending on the amount of tissue torn. The severe injury includes complete ligament rupture. The stretching or tearing is usually on the outside of the ankle, caused by the foot rolling under.

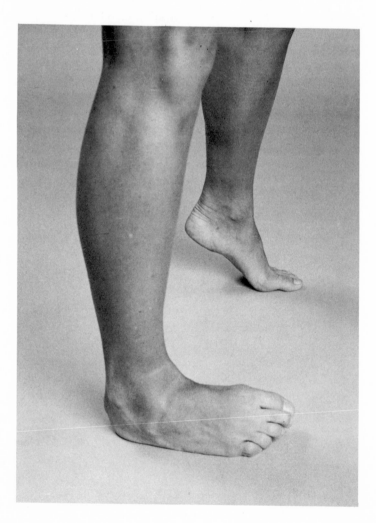

Mild sprains may require no delay in your game, but the moderate and severe injuries demand rest. For any significant sprain—one manifested by pain with weight bearing, swelling and tenderness—it is wise to elevate the leg, apply ice, and rest for several hours. One can usually determine then whether continued rest and a supporting bandage will be needed, or a visit to your doctor for more definitive care. This care might include x-rays, strapping, crutches or even a cast. Healing time depends on the extent of injury, and may vary from two days to two months.

For the moderate or severe injury, a rehabilitation program will be required to regain motion and strengthen supporting muscle. Return to tennis gradually. Begin on a backboard, then rally, and finally take on an opponent.

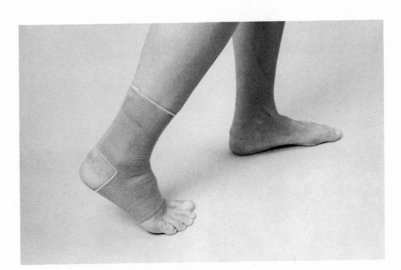

THE CALF, ANKLE AND FOOT

An elastic bandage or support provides only minimal support; however, ankle taping is effective for support if done correctly.

(1) (2)

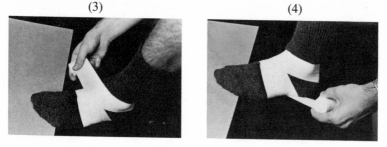

(3) (4)

(5) (6)

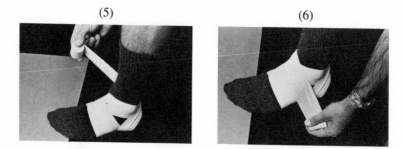

(7)

(8)

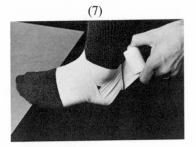
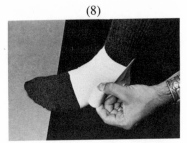

(9)

(10)

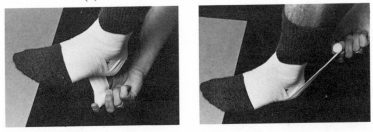

(11)

(12)

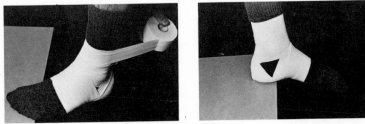

THE CALF, ANKLE AND FOOT

Your tennis shoe is important. It must fit well, have a good sole which is not too spongy or thick, and minimize slippage of the foot. Any shoe that feels "roly-poly" will likely lead to a sprain.

A second problem is called "weak ankle" and is caused by old ankle sprains, inherited loose supporting tissues, and inadequate muscle support. In this condition, the foot rolls over easily, leading to further tissue tearing.

Strengthening of the calf and foot muscles will help, but good shoes and ankle taping will be more helpful. Thin soled shoes such as worn by a boxer will give a more stable base.

As in other areas, local points of pain and tenderness can be caused by inflamed tendons or ligaments. If one week of rest doesn't solve the problem, your physician may use anti-inflammatory medicine by mouth, physical therapy (such as ultrasound) or a cortisone injection.

Degenerative or "wear and tear" changes in the joint can lead to swelling, stiffness, and aching. If a reduction in playing time doesn't solve the problem, it should be investigated by your physician. Strapping or taping can be helpful.

The Foot.   Many foot problems plague the tennis player, the most common involving the arch. The supporting tissue around the long arch becomes overloaded with resulting soreness and aching. Because the arch does not collapse with increasing age, there is no such condition as "fallen arch." Symptoms appear after prolonged play and are relieved by rest.

Tennis playing time can be increased by providing more support to your arch. This can be done by wearing a good tennis shoe with a built-in arch support, or by adding a support to your shoe. A good example is the Hopad® felt support, which is inexpensive, easy to use and available in several sizes. More formal appliances can be purchased or custom-made.

Foot and calf strengtening exercises will reduce the workload on the joints and connective tissue and should be done on a regular basis.

"Heel spur" pain occurs on the weight bearing surface of the heel. It is an inflammation at the attachment of the plantar fascia to the heel bone. This fascia runs under the long arch, much as a bow string. The pain is worse on weight bearing after rest, the pain decreasing as weight bearing continues.

Rest allows the inflammation to subside, but sometimes incompletely. A ¾" foam rubber heel pad helps remove stress, and should be worn in every shoe. With persisting pain, your physician will employ the same treatment as for other inflamed areas.

The area behind the heel may develop a bursitis from pressure or rubbing on your shoe; or inflammation may occur where the Achilles tendon attaches to the heel. Proper shoe fit is essential to prevent or treat this condition. During the acute phase, all pressure must be off the heel.

Pain and soreness under the metatarsal heads (forefoot fat pad) is also caused by too much pressure. Two of the causes include prominence of the metatarsal head with associated callus, and shrinkage of the fat pad with age, yielding inadequate bony protection.

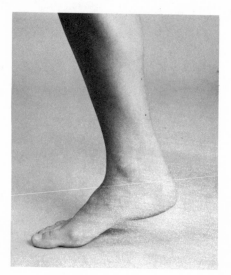

More padding under the forefoot is required. This can take the form of thicker soles, foam insole, longitudinal arch support or, in the more resistant types, a custom-made appliance. The latter can be moved to any shoe.

As with the fibula, prolonged foot stress can lead to metatarsal fatigue fracture. Soreness and forefoot swelling is the result. Three to six weeks rest are required. Sometimes strapping, casting or crutches will be needed.

Painful "corns" or "bunions" require more precise shoe fitting, the former more "toe box" height, and the latter more width. The severe bunion or corn problem can be helped by surgery.

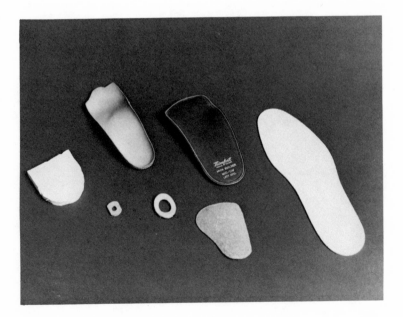

Blistering is produced by friction within the shoe, and is aggravated by moisture. It can be resolved only by preventing the foot from sliding and by reducing wetness. Correct shoe fit and adequate sock weight are imperative. Wool and cotton are absorbent, and therefore superior to the synthetic materials. There is no way to decrease your basic wetness, but by wearing shoes that breathe well, you will at least not add to the problem. Those whose feet do get very moist should change their socks frequently and use shoes with a terry cloth insole.

Pressure on a toe or along the margin of the foot can be caused by the edge of a narrow insole. This will produce a very tender bruised area. The solution is to find an insole as long and as wide as your foot. The "last" or outline of the shoe must correspond to your foot. Rubbing and pressure on the great toenail edge produces "tennis toe" with mild changes of irritation to the nail bed or bleeding under the nail. The latter

produces a throbbing pain and a purple-blue nail. Tennis toe is prevented by having an adequately fitting shoe. That includes (1) one in which you cannot slide lengthwise; (2) sufficient "toe-sox" height to clear the big toenail and (3) adequate length. Mild problems require only rest, but throbbing pain from bleeding under the nail needs relief by decompressing the blood collection by drilling a hole in the nail—best leave that to your doctor.

Some players have decreased mobility in the large joint at the base of their great toe. The demands of tennis produce a soreness in this joint which will intensify with continued play. More rigidity in the sole of the shoe is required. Slow down your game, stay down more on your heels, and play more doubles. In severe cases, surgery is helpful.

THE CALF, ANKLE AND FOOT

The greater the lateral contact of your shoe, the more stable the base. Avoid roly-poly shoes.

Remember that your physician can help you solve many of these annoying problems.

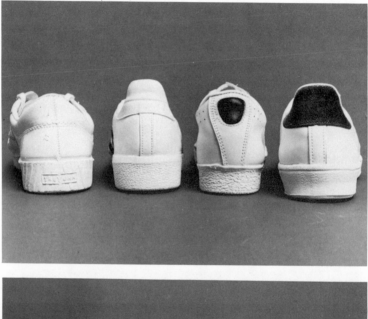

HEAT STROKE AND FLUID INTAKE

The body learns to accommodate to physical activity performed in hot weather, but it takes one to two weeks for the adjustment. During that interval, considerable salt (electrolytes) are lost along with the water in perspiration. This causes havoc, because a proper balance of potassium and sodium is essential for our well-being, and these are lost. The result is heatstroke.

Symptons of heatstroke are dizziness, headache, and upset stomach progressing to delirium, temperature elevation and fainting. In extreme cases, prostration, rapid pulse, hc dry skin and unconsciousness can occur.

Treatment requires the immediate removal to a cool shady place, and a recumbent position. Fluids should be taken, and beverages containing electrolytes are desirable, although returning to a balanced electrolyte state will take several hours. Cool compresses are used. Rapid temperature reduction is required in a severe case.

Prevention includes being in good physical shape and initially shortening the playing time when the weather turns hot. Drink plenty of fluid before, during and after play. Salt tablets and electrolyte fluids take hours to be effective, and are no panacea for the problem. Conditioning and fluids are the answer.

Muscle cramps are caused by the accumulation of waste products in the muscle, and by electrolyte imbalance. They therefore occur more often after prolonged vigorous play, and during hot weather. As in heatstroke, conditioning and fluids are vital. When cramps occur, massage, local heat, and stretching the muscle provide the best chance of resolution. If sufficiently severe, quit.

Exercises

Exercises are done to (1) warm up, (2) loosen up, (3) build muscle, (4) prevent injury, and (5) rehabilitate an injured area.

Since most of the conditions and injuries we have described relate to what we have called the "connective tissue," it is logical to spend our precious time on a priority system, with the prime emphasis on stretching. This will help protect from tearing or inflaming the tendons, fascia and ligaments.

Remember that your activities of daily living do not include the reaching, bending, twisting and lunging that occur in tennis.

Our second emphasis will be on strengthening muscle. The more muscle we have, the better we protect our joints, the harder we contact the ball, the faster we move and the greater our endurance.

Muscle strengthening exercises are isotonic, that is, moving the muscle to be exercised, or isometric, contracting the muscle against resistance without motion occurring. One muscle, a muscle group, or many muscles can be exercised at one time. The isometric exercises presented here concentrate on individual muscles, as does the isotonic program.

The beauty of isometric and stretching exercises is that they can be done anywhere, anytime and with no special equipment or help. For those who need or want company, nice surroundings and equipment, I have no objection to a health spa, athletic club, or well-equipped gym. The important object is to do the exercises regularly and in the correct way. There is no excuse for not developing a program to fit your time and physical attributes.

Warming Up Exercises

These are done immediately before play, just as a runner, gymnast or ballet dancer would warm up. They serve to stretch the connective tissue, which tightens during periods of rest, and to organize the entire body physiologically to the greater activity of play. The latter means (1) metabolic readiness to consume more oxygen; (2) neuromuscular readiness to reduce reflex time; (3) physic readiness as it relates to confidence and being alert.

The warm up exercises mentioned here are more fully described in the section on stretching exercises. The list below should take no more than three minutes of your time, when adequately learned. They must be done easily and in a relaxed state of mind.

Before leaving home, do ten of the lumbar back stretches. You can do these on or near the court if you don't embarrass easily. Remember, if you play early in the day, a warm shower one hour before your playing time will loosen your tight connective tissue extremely well.

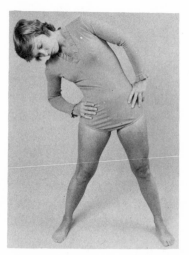

On the court or in the locker room, do five neck turns and neck bends. Then with your arms overhead, stretch them backward to aid in loosening the area around the shoulders. With your arms horizontal, rotate your trunk and arms clockwise and counterclockwise. With your hands on hips, alternately bend your trunk to the right and left. Follow this with twenty jumping jacks. Then while sitting on the edge of a bench, stretch down toward your toes with extended arms,

keeping your knees straight. At arm's length from a wall, slowly lean into the wall, gradually bending your elbows, keeping your body straight and your heels flat. Now standing

with the legs about 30″ apart, toes pointing directly forward and your hands on hips, slowly lean to the right while bending the right knee, and repeat this toward the left.

WARMING UP EXERCISES

If you have a minor "tennis elbow" problem, hold your racquet arm at shoulder level in front of your body with the elbow straight. With your hand clenched, flex the wrist as far as possible. Return the wrist to its neutral position, and alternately turn the arm inward with a flexed wrist, and then outward with an extended wrist.

Remember you need more warming up on cold or windy days. Protect yourself with sweat clothes or a warm sweater before and after play.

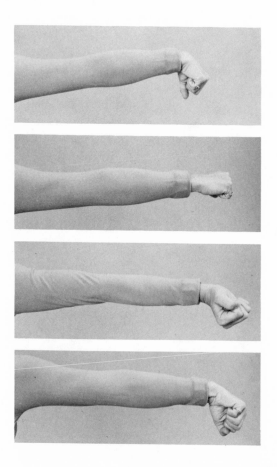

Stretching Exercises to Loosen Up

To prevent injury and gain greater freedom of movement, these are the most important of the exercises. People are born with a varying degree of connective tissue tightness. Those fortunate enough to be limber will be able to spend more of their time on muscle strengthening than on this stretching program. Remember that everyone becomes "stiffer" as one ages, as you have undoubtedly found after a demanding weekend of gardening or vigorous sport activity which you have not done on a regular basis. Remember also that you are more limber during the second half of the day and in warmer weather—factors which will influence your warm up time and the ability to perform the stretching exercises.

Tennis is a sport of movement, and these exercises are designed to give your joints greater mobility.

The exercises are listed anatomically. Not all need be done by everyone. They are to be done slowly and within the comfort range of the tissue being stretched. Go to the point of tightness and don't "bounce." Relax while holding the stretched position. Try to go a little farther each time. Stop the stretch if you experience pain. Don't try them on first awakening in the morning. Wait an hour, or take a warm shower first.

Hold the stretched position for five seconds, and repeat each stretch five to ten times, twice a day if possible.

The Neck

Here we are only concerned with side bending and rotation.

Side Bending.   With your head erect, eyes level, try to place the right ear on the right shoulder. (Don't raise the shoulder!) You may increase the stretch by reaching over your head with your right hand and try to pull the head toward the right, and repeat to the left.

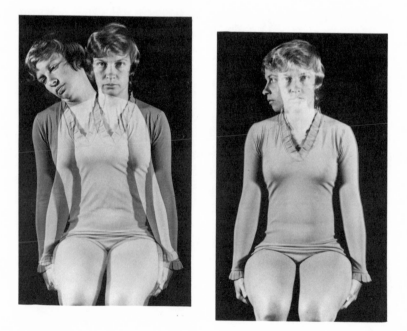

Rotation.   With your head erect, eyes level, turn your face and try to look over your right shoulder as far as possible. Additional stretch can be accomplished by cupping the left hand and applying pressure to the chin. Repeat to the left.

The Shoulders

Overhead Stretch. Bring arms overhead into the diving position with elbows straight. Stretch arms backward as far as possible.

Horizontal Rotary Stretch. Standing with arms horizontal at shoulder level, cross them in front, then out to the side and back as far as possible.

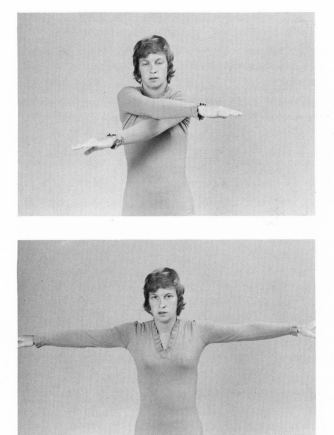

THE SHOULDERS

NOTE: If there is any problem with shoulder tendinitis or bursitis, omit the previous exercise and substitute the one following:

Standing with arms in tight to body and elbows bent to 90 degrees, hands pointing straight ahead, slowly turn arms so hand points out to the side. Now rest your arms at the side, turn the arm and bend the elbow, slowly reaching up behind the back to scratch the spine as high as possible with the tip of your thumb.

(1)

(2)

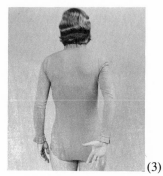

(3)

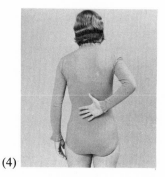

(4)

Avoid the football throwing position if you have shoulder bursitis or tendinitis

Anterior Shoulder Stretch. Lying on your back with your legs together and knees bent, a small rolled towel between your shoulder blades, clasp your hands behind your head and slowly flatten your elbows to the floor.

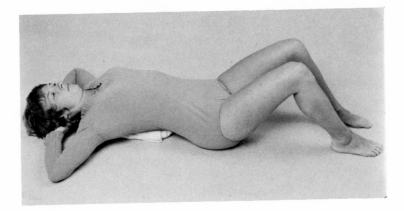

WRIST

Wrist

Extension.   Standing by a table with palm flat on surface, extend the wrist by bringing the forearm to the vertical position without raising the palm.

Flexion.   Standing with arms horizontal in front, elbows straight and a tight fist, slowly flex the wrist while the palm is down. Increase stretch by pressure from the opposite hand over the knuckles.

Rotation.   In the same position as for flexion stretch, slowly turn the wrist and arm inward, and then outward.

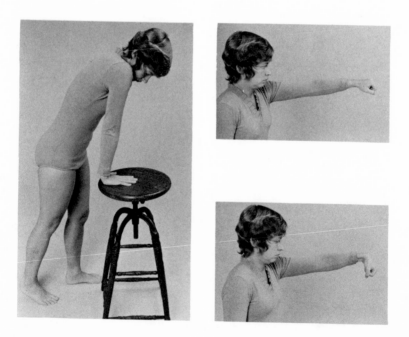

Dorsal Spine

Bending.   Stand with feet apart and hands on hips. Slowly bend your trunk to the right, then repeat to the left.

Rotation.   Standing with your legs crossed, feet flat on the floor and hands clasped behind your head, rotate your trunk and shoulders as far as you can to the right. Repeat to the left.

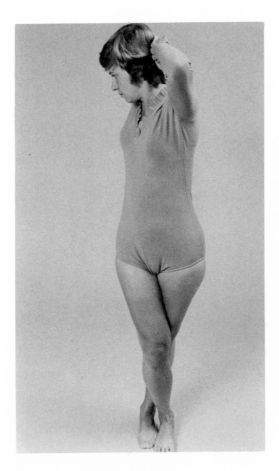

Lumbar Spine

Flexion Stretches.   Lying on your back with knees flexed and together, feet flat on the floor, grasp legs below knees and slowly raise the knees toward the chest. Keep your head down. When this is easily performed, repeat but bring the head up and between the knees.

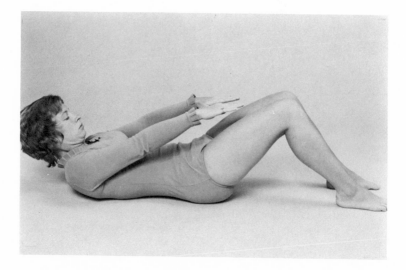

From the "long sitting" position, stretch arms down the legs as far as possible. When easily performed, bring your forehead down toward your knees.

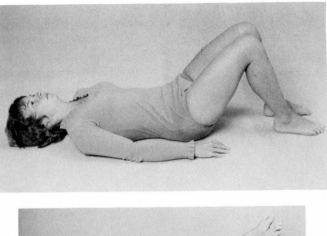

Hips

Extension.   Bend over a kitchen counter, flex one knee and grasp the foot with the hand on the same side. Pull the foot upward and backward while slowly bringing your body erect. Repeat on the opposite side. Be careful if you have low back problems.

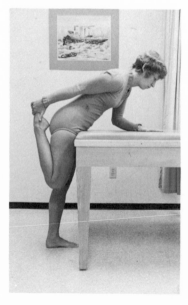 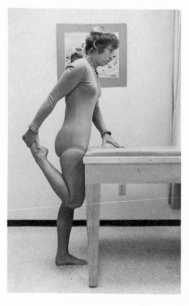

Abduction.   Standing with legs 24″ to 30″ apart, toes pointed ahead, hands on hips, slowly bend the right knee while leaning toward the right. Repeat to the left. Keep your trunk upright.

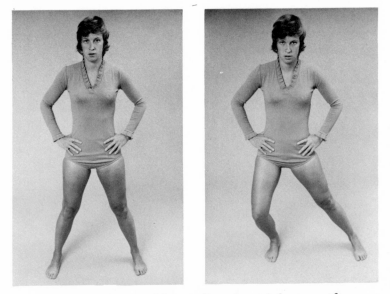

Sitting with hips and knees flexed, with knees wide apart and soles of feet together, push down on the knees with your hands until you feel tightness in the inner thigh region.

The same may be repeated while lying on your back.

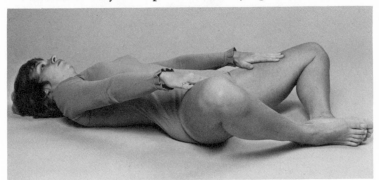

Thigh

Hamstring Stretch.   Sitting on the edge of a chair or bench with knees straight, slowly reach down the legs with the extended arms.

In the "long sitting" position, slowly reach down toward your toes with the extended arms. (This can be performed quite well in a warm tub.)

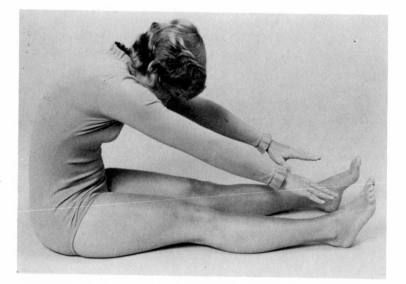

Calf

Heel Cord Stretch.   Stand facing the wall at arm's length, toes pointing forward, slowly bend the elbows while leaning toward the wall, keep the body straight and the heels flat on the floor.

CALF

Stand on the edge of a stair, heels over the edge, let the calf muscles fully relax so the heels sag down. This can also be done one foot at a time.

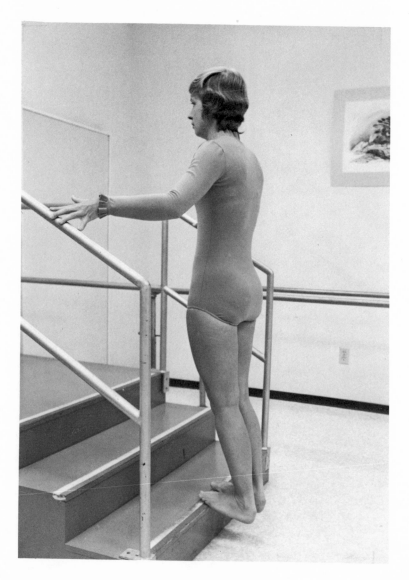

Stand at arm's length from a counter or high table, right knee straight and behind, left leg forward with knee flexed. Slowly lean toward the table, bending the elbows and the left knee while keeping the right knee straight and the right heel down. Repeat with right leg forward.

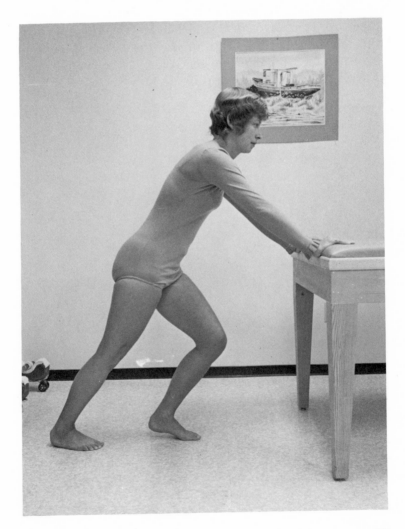

ANKLE

Ankle

After a moderate or severe sprain, there is usually some residual tightness which can be overcome by a stretching program.

Sitting with the affected foot over the opposite knee, grasp your heel with the opposite hand and the forefoot with the other hand. Slowly turn the heel and forefoot inward so you can see the sole. Then turn the heel and forefoot outward. Now pull the heel up, while gently forcing the forefoot down. Always stop at the point of pain.

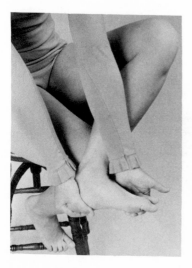

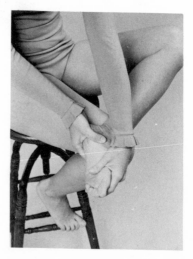

Toes

In the same cross-legged position as for the ankle stretch, grasp the toes with the same hand and apply a downward (flexion) force at the base of the toes. For increased forefoot flexibility, practice dropping your tennis socks and picking them up with your toes.

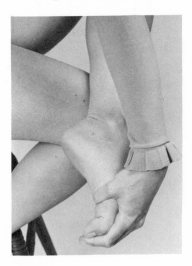

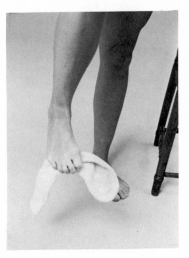

Muscle Strengthening Exercises

As previously mentioned, muscles can be strengthened by moving them against resistance, or contracting one system of muscles against another with no motion occurring. The former are isotonic and the latter isometric exercises.

In the isometric program, we hold the resistance for a period of time, rest for a prescribed time, and do a certain number of repetitions. Build up the contraction to almost maximal, hold for five seconds (count 1001, 1002 etc.), rest between contractions for five seconds. Initially repeat the contractions five times. Gradually increase to ten times. These exercises can be done more than one time a day, and in almost any location or position.

Neck, trunk and shoulder isometric exercises are described first, followed by specific isotonic and isometric exercises for the arms and legs.

Isometric Exercises

Neck.
1. Push with the base of your palm against the side of your head above your ear. Resist any motion by keeping your head erect.
2. With palms together on the forehead, push hands backward. Resist any motion by keeping the head erect.
3. With fingers interlocked, hands behind head, pull hands forward, again preventing motion by keeping head erect.

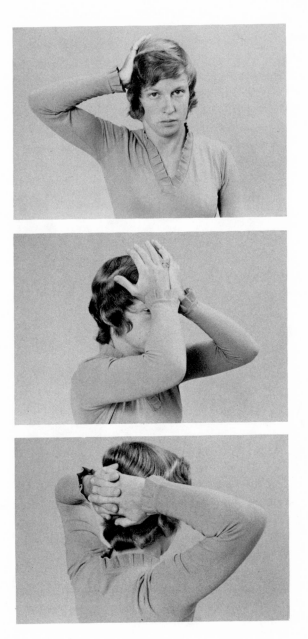

Dorsal Area.

1. Lie on your stomach with a small pillow under your hips and your arms at your side. Keeping chin tucked, raise your head and shoulders as high as possible. Don't hold your breath. Begin doing this three times, and with practice increase to ten times. Hold the elevated position for a slow . . . count with equal rest time between.

2. Lying on your stomach with arms stretched 45 degrees overhead, lift your arms . . . inches off the floor and hold them in the elevated position for a slow count of . . . With practice, increase to a count of . . . Relax for an equal amount of time. Initially repeat five times, work up to ten.

   CAUTION: These last two exercises are difficult for anyone with a low back pain problem. If they cause low back discomfort, stop them at once.

Lumbar Area. The first exercise listed under "dorsal area" is also excellent for strengthening the lumbar musculature. However, those with low back pain problems may not be able to do this exercise.

Trunk Muscles

Side Bends. Standing with legs apart, hands on hips, slowly bend your body to the right. Hold this position for a count of . . . Repeat to the left. Rest between bends. Begin with three repetitions and gradually increase to ten.

Opposite Arm and Leg Lifts. While lying face down with a pillow under your hips, raise the right leg and left arm simultaneously. Repeat with the left leg and the right arm. Hold for a count of . . ., rest between lifts. Five repetitions.

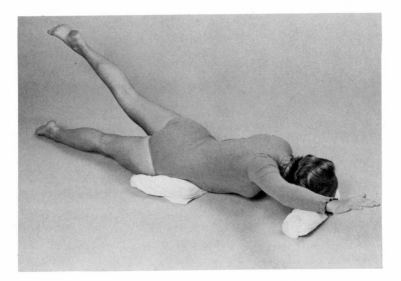

ABDOMINAL MUSCLES

Abdominal Muscles

Partial Sit-up.   Lying on your back with legs together and knees bent, feet tucked under a piece of furniture, slowly sit up halfway by initially flexing the neck, then lifting the shoulder off the floor. Continue curling the body until your hands touch the top of your knees. Hold for a count of . . . Slowly uncurl. Rest between sit-ups. Begin with five sit-ups and slowly increase the number to twenty.

This and the following exercise are partially isotonic.

Diagonal Sit-up.   In the same starting position as "partial sit-up" but with hands entwined behind your head, elbows wide apart, slowly curl your body into a partial sit-up while turning to the left, bringing the right elbow to the outside of the rasied left knee. Hold for a count of . . . Slowly unwind and uncurl. Repeat to the right. Rest, and then repeat as with partial sit-ups.

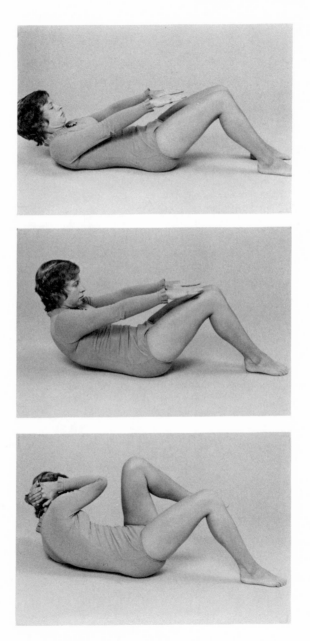

SHOULDERS

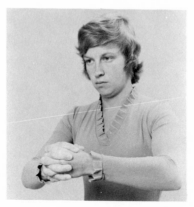

Shoulders

Arm Pull.   Stand with right arm at your side, grasp the right wrist with your left hand. Pull down on the right arm while preventing motion by resisting with the right shoulder muscles. Repeat on the left side.

Pectoral Strengthening.   Standing with arms bent in front at shoulder level, push the left fist into the right palm, resisting with the right arm. Repeat with right fist in left palm.

Deltoid and Scapular Stretch.   In the same position as above but with fingers tightly entwined, try to pull your hands apart.

85

SHOULDER

Isotonic Exercises

Progressive resistance exercises (P.R.E.) can be done with graduated weights in a gymnasium, health spa, therapy center, or at home. Dumbbell weight of 3#, 5# and 10# are excellent to have at home to strengthen the shoulders, arms, forearms and wrists. Begin with the 3# dumbbell weight, increase to 5# and then 10# as the exercise becomes easy.

Shoulder Shrug.   With dumbbell weights in both hands, arms at side and elbows straight, slowly elevate or shrug shoulders. Hold the elevated position for a slow count of . . . relax, and repeat ten times.

Deltoid Strengthening.   With 3# dumbbell weights in both hands at the sides, slowly bring the weights in front to shoulder level with palms facing down. Hold for a slow . . . count. Bring the arms slowly down and relax. Begin with five repetitions. Gradually increase to twenty repetitions.

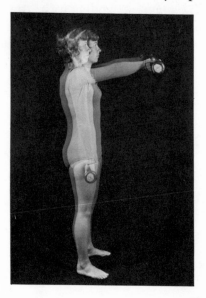

Middle Deltoid. Repeat the above exercise, but bring the arms out horizontally to the side.

The crawl and backstroke in swimming, as well as push-ups and pull-ups, are excellent means of developing the shoulder muscles.

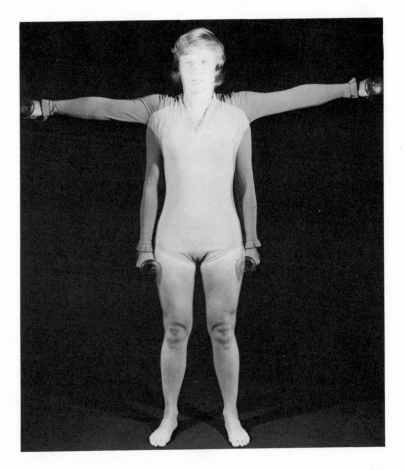

SHOULDER

Shoulder Relaxation. To relieve tightness and tension around the neck and shoulders, slowly shrug the shoulders in a rotating fashion, first forward and then backward. Keep your chin tucked.

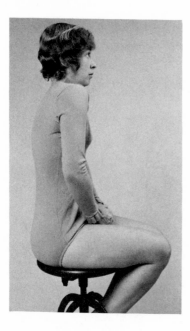

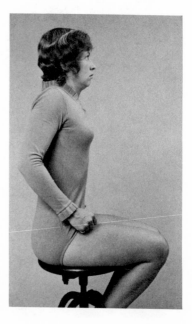

Arm

Triceps. *Isometric:* Standing with arms in front at waist level, elbows bent, put right fist into the cupped left hand. Push down with the right arm while resisting with the left. Reverse hand positions. This exercise will simultaneously work the triceps of the right arm and the biceps of the left.

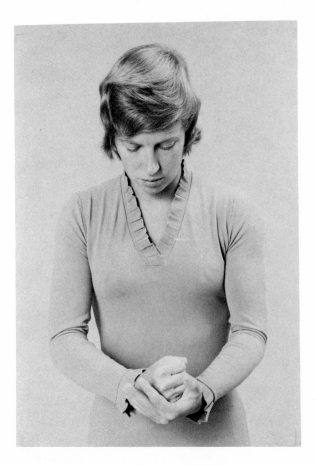

ARM

P.R.E.: Lie in bed face down, with right· elbow bent and forearm hanging over the side, 3# dumbbell weight in hand. Slowly straighten the elbow, hold for the count of . . . slowly bend the elbow. Increase weight and repetitions as with shoulder dumbbell exercises.

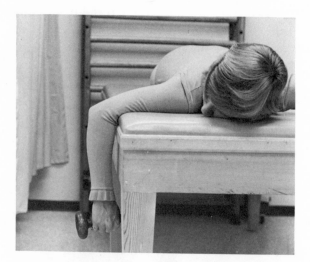

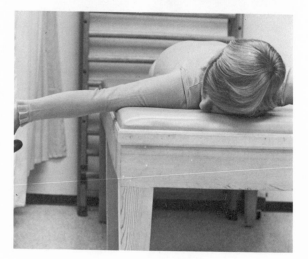

Biceps.   *Isometric:*   Use the same exercise as for isometric triceps, above.

P.R.E.:   Standing with a 3# dumbbell in one or both hands, palm facing up, slowly flex your elbow(s). Increase weight and repetition as for triceps and shoulder strengthening.

Pull-ups are excellent for biceps strengthening.

FOREARM AND HAND

Forearm and Hand

Isometric: Clasp hands in front at waist level. Squeeze top of the opposite hand with the fingers as hard as possible, and in the same position try to turn the left forearm as though the left palm were going to be turned downward. Resist with the right hand so that no motion occurs. Repeat, trying to turn the palm upward.

Note: Avoid these 2 exercises if you have arthritis of fingers.

P.R.E.: Sit with the right forearm along the arm of a table or chair with the wrist over the front edge, palm down, 3# dumbbell grasped in hand. Slowly raise the wrist as high as possible. Repeat with the palm turned up. Use the same weight and repetition program as for shoulder or biceps P.R.E.

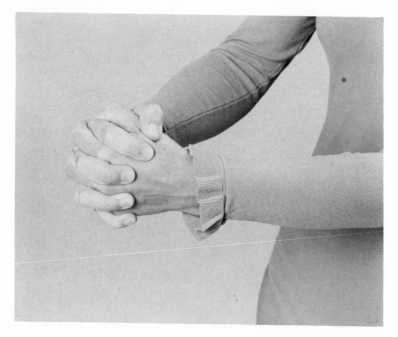

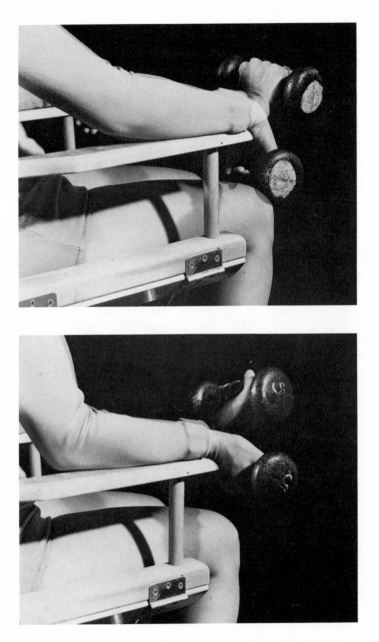

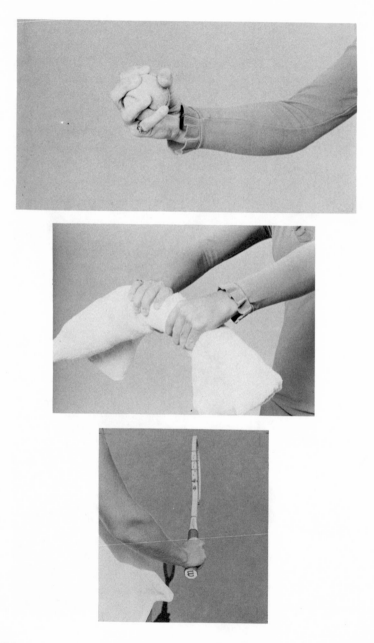

FOREARM AND HAND

For greater stretching force, the above P.R.E. exercises can be done with the arm horizontal in front with the elbow straight.

Squeeze a tennis ball or spring grip slowly and rhythmically twenty times.

Practice wringing out a terry cloth towel.

Practice squeezing your tennis racquet grip.

THIGH

Thigh

Hamstrings and Gluteals:.   Isotonic: Lie on stomach with a
small pillow under your hips, with legs straight. Raise one leg
8-10″ and hold for a slow 3 count. Bring the leg down slowly
and relax. Begin with three repetitions, and slowly increase to
ten.

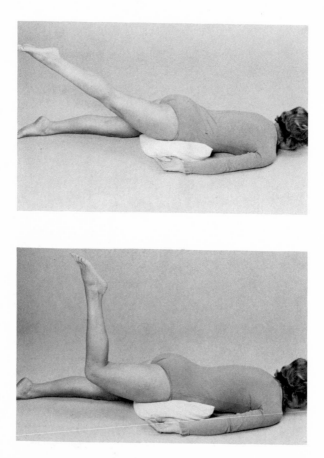

From the same position but with one knee bent to 70
degrees, as illustrated, repeat the same exercise.

Isometric: Standing with one heel hooked under the edge of a heavy chair, slowly attempt to raise the chair with the heel.

Sitting with the heel hooked over the arm of a couch, try to flex the leg by pulling the heel against the edge of the couch.

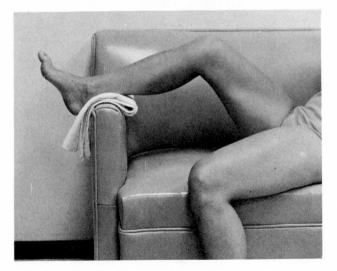

THIGH

Quadriceps.   *Isometric:*   Sit, leaning back with the right heel resting on the floor, left foot crossed over the right ankle. Try to raise the right heel off the floor while resisting with the left leg.

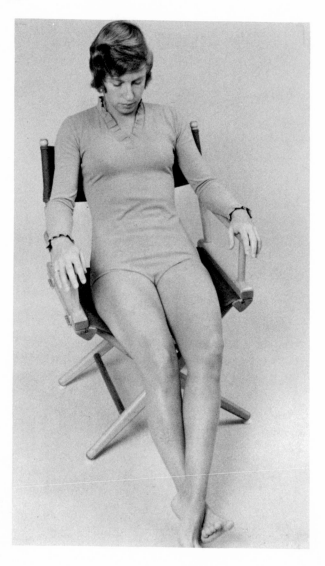

Sit against the wall with the knees bent to 90 degrees. Hold for 5 count. Gradually increase the amount of time. Skiers call this the "phantom chair."

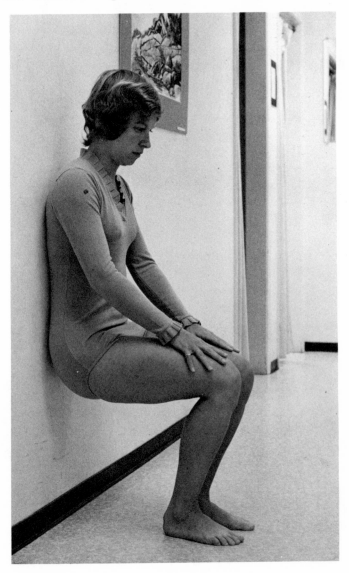

THIGH

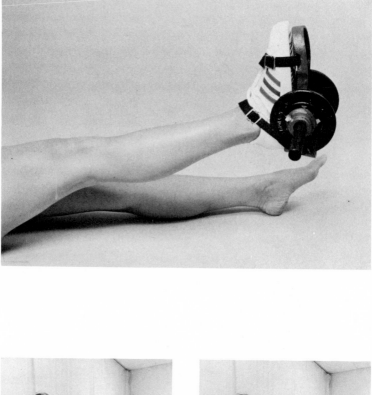

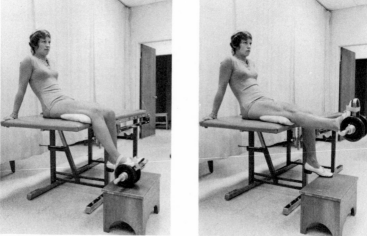

P.R.E.: "Long sitting" on the floor, attach 5# of weight to the right shoe. Slowly raise the right leg while counting to 3. Hold for a 3 count, and slowly relax. Initially repeat ten times, gradually increase to twenty. When one weight level becomes easy, increase the weight by 2# increments as high as practical.

Sitting on a high table with a small pillow under the distal thigh, add 5# of weight to the right shoe or foot. Slowly straighten the right knee while counting 3. Hold for a slow count of 3, and slowly relax. In the relaxed position, a stool under the right leg should remove the pull of the weight. Repeat and increase the weights as in the "long sitting" position. Do not do this exercise if you have a kneecap problem.

Shoe weights and ankle weights can be purchased from a sports equipment store. Improvised weights can be made at home by using a bag or purse filled with sand, bricks, books, or cans.

Calf

Posterior Muscles.　　*Isotonic:*　　Stand with one foot flat and the other slightly raised from the floor. Lightly balance yourself with fingers on a wall or table. Slowly rise as high on the ball of your foot as possible. Hold for a 3 count. Slowly relax. Repeat ten times, gradually increase the number of repetitions to thirty.

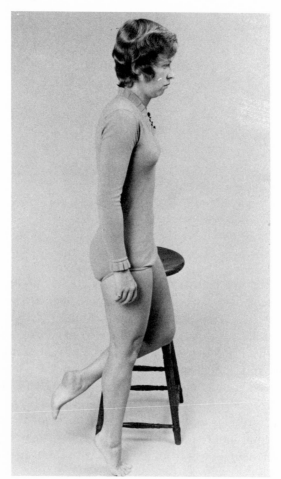

This may be combined with Achilles tendon stretching by standing on the edge of a stair and alternately sagging then rising up onto the ball of the foot. Try it one foot at a time for greater stretch and strength.

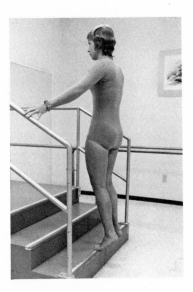

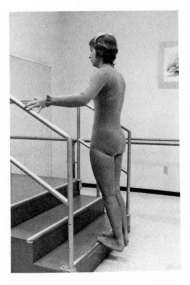

CALF

Shin and Lateral Calf.   *Isometric:*   Lying down on your back with knees straight, cross the ball of the left foot over onto the right forefoot. Pull up the right ankle while resisting with the left foot. Reverse positions, and repeat as with other isometric exercises.

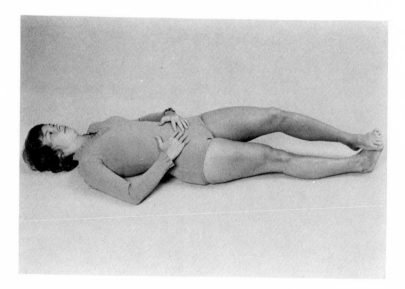

Therapeutic or Rehabilitative Exercises

These are exercises prescribed by your doctor or recommended by a therapist. They will be prescribed following injury, operation or episode of severe inflammation. Examples of such use would include exercises for the arm after a fracture of the forearm, exercises for the thigh after a knee operation, or a specific shoulder exercise regimen after a severe case of bursitis. Although many of the exercises previously described might be beneficial to your rehabilitation, the exercise program must be tailored to you and your problem. It is therefore essential that the prescription be given by your physician. Don't quit early. Wait until your doctor or therapist is satisfied. Inadequate rehabilitation will not only make tennis more difficult and less fun, but will make other activities of daily living much harder. Complete your program. Don't allow the rest of your body to tighten and weaken, continue with a daily stretching program and as many general exercises such as swimming or cycling as your doctor will allow.

You will be amazed how your body will respond to a regular program of exercise. The reward will be better tennis with fewer aches and pains.

Glossary of Terms

anterior: In front of (the arm, leg or body).

bones:

    humerus: upper arm bone.

    radius: outer forearm bone.

    ulna: inner forearm bone.

    carpal: any of eight wrist bones.

    scaphoid: vulnerable carpal bone at base of thumb.

    Metacarpals: bones of the hand between carpals and phalanges, five in all, one going to each finger.

    phalanges: bones of the fingers, fourteen in all.

    vertebrae: components of the backbone; both moveable ones, in the cervical, dorsal and lumbar spine, and the immobile sacrum and the coccyx.

    femur: the large thigh bone.

    patella: kneecap.

    tibia: major bone of calf.

    fibula: small outer calf bone.

    tarsal: bones of the instep, seven in all.

    metatarsal: five bones of the forefoot.

bursa: fluid filled sac, formed in areas of pressure over a bone or where a tendon rides over a bone, and elsewhere.

capsule: membrane surrounding a joint.

connective tissue: the general supporting or uniting tissue of the body, includes ligament, bursa, fascia, capsule, tendon lining, etc.

cortisone: a steroid drug used as an anti-inflammatory medicine.

disc: cushion between vertebral bodies.

Dupuytren's contracture: tightening and thickening of the fascial tissue in the palm, often causing the fingers to be pulled down.

epicondyle: projection from a long bone usually near the joint; common attachment for muscles.

extension: refers to the straightening of a joint.

fascia: a sheet of fibrous tissue under the skin and surrounding muscle.

flexion: refers to the bending of a joint.

frozen shoulder: limitation of shoulder joint motion often occurring after tendinitis.

ganglion: cystic swelling from a joint lining or tendon sheath.

isometric: exercise by muscle contraction without motion.

isotonic: exercise by muscle contraction with motion and against a weight.

itis: a suffix denoting inflammation.

joint: moveable union between two bones.

ligament: a band of fibrous tissue connecting two bones.

lumbar: the part of the back between the ribs and the pelvis; the loins.

meniscus: cartilage in a semilunar shape attached to the joint surface at the knee; each knee has two, medial and lateral.

muscles:

   abductor: muscles pulling away from the midline; our reference here is to those on either side of the pelvis pulling the legs apart.

   adductor: muscles pulling toward the midline; we are referring to those in the groin pulling the legs together.

   anterior tibial: muscle of the anterior shin which pulls the foot up.

   biceps: referring to the anterior upper arm muscle which bends the elbow.

   deltoid: large lateral shoulder muscle which elevates the arm.

   extensors: muscles which straighten a joint.

   flexors: muscles which bend a joint.

gastrocnemius: large posterior calf muscle, attaches to Achilles tendon and plantar flexes the foot.

gluteus: large buttock and lateral pelvic muscles which straighten or abduct (see above) the hip.

hamstring: one of several large posterior thigh muscles which bend the knee.

paraspinals: those muscles running along the spine and helping to keep it erect.

pronator: forearm muscle which rotates the radius so the palm turns down (as seen with the elbow bent).

quadriceps: group of four anterior thigh muscles which extend the knee; the patella rests in its tendon at the knee.

supinator: forearm muscles which rotate the radius so the palm turns up (as seen with the elbow bent).

triceps: muscle group behind the upper arm which extends the elbow.

orthopedic: the branch of surgery that treats diseases and injuries of the bones and joints.

"pinched nerve:" irritation of, or pressure on, a nerve, usually near the spinal cord where the nerve goes through a bony tunnel.

plantar: relating to the sole of the foot.

posterior: refers to the back of the arm, leg or body.

pronation: the act of turning the forearm so the palm faces backward or down.

shoe last: the outline of the inner sole of the shoe.

"slipped disc:" a rupture of the fibrocartilaginous cushion between the vertebra so that some of the material is displaced.

supination: the act of turning the forearm so the palm faces forward or upward.

synovium: the secreting membrane lining a joint, tendon or bursa.

tendon: a fibrous cord or band connecting a muscle with its bony attachment.

toe box: upper portion of the front end of a shoe.

"trigger finger:" inflammation of a tendon where it goes through a fibrous sheath or tunnel, the result is a locking of a finger in flexion with sudden giving away into extension, hence "triggering."

ultrasound: technique of delivering sound waves into the tissue, often with resultant decrease in inflammation.

BOOKS OF RELATED INTEREST

In BEYOND JOGGING: The Innerspaces of Running, Michael Spino brings together spiritual concepts such as meditation and body awareness with the physical techniques of Olympic coaches to make a creative, self-actualizing experience. "After Mike Spino, running will never be the same. . ." (George Leonard) 128 pages, soft cover, $3.95

SKATEBOARDING by Jack Grant is the first complete guide to this fad-turned-major-sport. Riding positions and major tricks are extensively illustrated and the concise text covers everything from fundamentals to safety. 96 pages, soft cover, $3.95

Jerry Colleto's YOGA CONDITIONING AND FOOTBALL presents a revolutionary new approach to conditioning for athletes and general fitness for everyone. 112 pages, soft cover, $3.95

In THE WORLD OF WOMEN'S GYMNASTICS, Jim Gault and Jack Grant have written a stimulating, insightful, and extraordinarily instructional overview of the sport. Gymnasts, coaches, judges, parents, teachers, and enthusiastic spectators will all learn from it---and love it. 144 pages, soft cover, $3.95

BICYCLE MOTOCROSS: ACOMPLETE GUIDE by Ted Wise contains information on equipment, tracks, safety, tricks, jumps, sanctioning organizations, racing psychology, practice and maintenance for America's fastest growing new sport. 128 pages, soft cover, $3.95

Charles Tips' FRISBEE BY THE MASTERS is the most complete and up-to-date book available, offering a step-by-step guide to 240 advanced Frisbee techniques. 144 pages, soft cover, $4.95

CELESTIAL ARTS
231 Adrian Road,
Millbrae, California 94030